Y0-CBF-220

LOOK HERE, LORD

LOOK HERE, LORD

MEDITATIONS FOR TODAY'S WOMAN

by

Clarissa Start

Illustrated by
Audrey F. Teeple

Augsburg Publishing House
Minneapolis   Minnesota

LOOK HERE, LORD

Copyright © 1972 Augsburg Publishing House
Library of Congress Catalog Card No. 72-78550
International Standard Book No. 0-8066-1218-5

Scripture quotations are from the Revised Standard Version of the Bible, copyright 1946 and 1952 by the Division of Christian Education of the National Council of Churches, and are used by permission.

All rights reserved. No part of this book may be used or reproduced in any manner whatsoever without written permission except in the case of brief quotations embodied in critical articles and reviews. For information address Augsburg Publishing House, 426 South Fifth Street, Minneapolis, Minnesota 55415.

Manufactured in the United States of America

CONTENTS

Look Here, Lord

Women take things personally.

A man once said this to his wife and she retorted, "Why Henry, I do not." Or so the story goes.

Perhaps the charge is true and women are too inclined to be subjective rather than objective. Certainly our lives are oriented to people—the people in our families, the people in our daily lives. Women deal with people.

Another joke has a husband saying, "I decide the big issues, such as should we recognize Red China, and my wife decides the little ones like what kind of house or car we buy." And there's much truth to that, too.

A woman is not only personal but innately possessive. She talks about "my husband," "my child," "my refrigerator," or even, "my arthritis."

Even today's liberated woman, a woman whose horizons go beyond the four walls of home, looks at the world in homey terms. If she's invited to the White House, she's thinking, "What pretty pink napkins," and "I wonder if she picks out his ties for him."

Inevitably some of this carries over into our religious life. A mother of simple faith looks up to the sky and says, "Take care of him," as her child starts to school. We know our prayers should be world wide in scope, yet we can't help praying for our home and our children and our families.

The woman writer—well, this woman writer, to make it personal—starts to write in generalities but ends up writing of things close to her heart and home.

Each of these meditations had its inspiration in something that happened to me in real life. Sometimes a happy happening. Sometimes one rooted in sorrow. But always personal.

A woman's conversations with God are like that, too. Personal. When she says, "Look here, Lord," she may do it in exasperation, as if calling him on the celestial carpet—usually because someone near and dear to her has been wronged, hurt, treated unfairly by an impersonal world.

But at other times, she says it humbly.

"Look here, Lord. Over here, in this small corner where I perform the routine duties of an unimportant life."

She says it in supplication.

Look here, Lord. I know you've had a busy day and I sympathize for I have busy days, too, but could you squeeze in one more thing. . . . I really need you now. . . . I've made such a mess of things. . . . Look at me, this least person. Forgive me. Straighten out my life. Give me direction. Give me purpose. Look here, Lord. Look at this woman. Make her over in your image. Make her a better person.

8

The Power
of Silence

A French writer tells the story of a country inn-keeper who noticed that a saint had registered at his desk. That night the thought occurred to him that it would be interesting to hear how a real saint said her prayers.

He tiptoed down the corridor and stood outside her room and listened. But the only sound he heard from behind the closed doors was a long silence, occasionally broken by the words, "Yes, Lord. . . . Yes, Lord. . . . Yes, Lord."

How different from the way most of us pray. For every one who says, "Speak, Lord; for thy servant hears," there must be ten who say, "Hear, Lord; for thy servant speaks."

I am one of the ten, I fear. My prayers are inclined to be detailed road maps for the Lord to follow. I have some definite ideas on what's wrong and right with the world and what should be changed, especially in my own life. Anyone listening outside my bedroom door after dark probably would hear me saying, "Now look here, Lord. . . ."

9

I do this in spite of incontrovertible evidence that my way is not always the best way. I have often bounced my head against a stone wall trying to break through, only to have an unseen door open quietly and provide the solution to my problem.

Sometimes my fondest wish has been answered, my request granted. (Perhaps, the Lord, like a husband nagged too long, has a tendency to say, "All right, all right, have it your way.") Later I found that what I thought I wanted wasn't what I wanted after all. Sometimes my prayerful request has been denied and I have later been tremendously thankful and relieved that it was.

One spring, at a church I attended, the minister suggested that most of us do too much talking instead of listening in our spiritual life. As an experiment, a period of silence was initiated before each church service during Lent. Those who chose to do so arrived half an hour early and simply sat in silence in the sanctuary.

My first experience with silent meditation was a little eerie. Aware that one should truly blank out one's mind, not think about a spring wardrobe or the day's menu, I tried, but it wasn't easy. Our world is geared to sound, not silence. But soon I discovered it was possible to give myself over to silence and that it can be a wonderful thing, a soft enveloping feeling, like watching a snowfall.

When the silent period was over, the doors swung open and people began coming in. There was a momentary feeling of shock; they were no noisier than usual but the shattering of the silence was an assault on the eardrums.

I wish I could say I initiated my own period of daily silence. I haven't achieved that yet. But now and then, after dark, in bed, out of doors on a beautiful sunny day, occasionally I do stop, listen, and try to say, "Yes, Lord. . . . Yes, Lord. . . . Yes, Lord."

Speak, Lord, for thy servant hears.   I Samuel 3:9

Lord, sainthood is far away for most of us. Our self-centered human nature makes us feel we know what is best. Teach us to pray . . . and sometimes not to pray aloud at all, but to listen . . . to make us aware of the great power that exists far beyond our finite powers. Teach us not to make outlines, but to wait for guidelines; to say not, "Listen here, Lord," but, "Speak, Lord, thy servant listens."

11

Why,
O Lord, Why?

The city of Hamburg was destroyed, much of it in a single bombing raid. Church visitors who toured the city after the war usually were taken to an enormous cemetery where row upon row of simple stone markers designate the graves. On many of them is a one word question, *"Warum?"*

Warum? W is pronounced with the sound of the English "V" and the *r* is spoken with a deep sonorous roll. *Warum?* It means, "Why?"

Why, O Lord, why? Why me? Why was I singled out for grief and sorrow and punishment?

The psalmist asked it, and men and women ask it every day. The man who has failed in his job. The couple who have given birth to a handicapped child. The widow, the widower who lost the person who should have been a life's companion for many more years. Why, O Lord, why?

I asked it myself when my husband died. Accusingly, reproachfully, bitterly, grievingly. Why me?

Some who ask the question never do answer it to their satisfaction, and all their days are tinged with bitterness. They were the pawns singled out on a checkerboard senselessly. Others grow painfully to maturity, and eventually the harsh cry of "Why?" takes on a different tone. It becomes a questioning, childlike query.

Why? Perhaps there was a reason. Perhaps all things do work together for good. Perhaps if we seek and ask and listen instead of accuse and rant and berate. . . .

Why, O Lord? Not angrily but questingly. Why did it happen?

Did you mean for me to do something else? Be someone else? Did you want me to be torn from my comfortable cocoon? Did you intend for me to feel pain and grow out of smugness and superficiality? If there was purpose beyond my tragedy, what was it?

Paul was struck blind on the road to Damascus and instead of asking, "Why?" asked, "What?" "What, O Lord, wilt thou have me to do?"

I asked this question and found some answers. I began to write for widows. In a small way, I have helped conduct retreats for the bereaved. Above all, I have found myself infinitely more aware of, more sensitive to those who have known loss. It is a slight contribution, but it is something.

Many persons of far greater fame—the Kennedy family, Dale Evans and Roy Rogers—have known the sorrow of a handicapped child and have channeled their sorrow into help for research and treatment of the handicapped, as well as serving as examples of courage for other parents. Art Linkletter lost a daughter through drugs and directed his energies to educating and helping other parents to live through—and avoid—his tragedy.

Not everyone has a talent, large or small, not everyone has resources to be of material aid, but everyone has the ability to raise his head from his own sorrow and reach out a hand to someone else who has known sorrow.

After asking, *"Warum? Why?"* After asking, "What? What can I do?" The person who has been struck down with sorrow can ask, "How?"

How can I help my fellow man?

Blessed are those who mourn,
for they shall be comforted.   Matthew 5:4

Lord, teach me to listen, to hear and accept your answer to my cry of "Why?" Then help me to fulfill your will.

14

The Organized Life

Every now and then the daily newspaper prints a story about a gory murder, with the routine observation, "Signs of a struggle were seen in every room of the house."

If ever I'm done in, I hope no one takes that line too seriously. There are times when my entire house shows "signs of struggle"—the struggle to clean it up and get it organized.

My favorite cartoon is one of two men with their feet on the same desk. Its caption, "Next week we've got to get organized." For a long time it hung over my office desk and reminded me, from time to time, to "get organized." My haphazard, part-time homemaking almost never makes the grade.

But not long ago we moved from one house to another and then we had to "get organized." We had to clean closets and shelves and drawers, and a great many things were pitched, including my priceless collection of funny birthday cards accumulated for 15 years.

There's tremendous therapy in cleaning out shelves and stripping yourself to bare essentials. Often, in throwing away pieces of paper, you throw away the bitterness and petty grudges and disturbing memories of other years. When you dig them out from the bottom of a drawer, you also dredge them up from the recesses of your subconscious and see them for what they were—pretty trivial.

For instance, among my souvenirs, I found carbon copies of memorandums to a boss I once had. The man was a little tyrant and, like most tyrants, he was eventually deposed. As I read the memos, I found myself smoldering anew over injustices, a little amused but also annoyed.

"How ridiculous!" I suddenly decided. "I'm letting myself get all upset again." And I consigned the papers to the wastebasket.

Another little gem I came across was a list titled, "Things That Keep Me Awake This Year of 1937." A long long time ago, 1937. Reading over the list of things that kept me awake, I found I might as well have gone to sleep. Not one had been more than a passing frenzy.

I worried—in that day of depression and hard times—about being fired from my mediocre job. I wasn't. Eventually I quit and found a better one. I worried over my mother's health. She lived for

30 more years and knew days of great vitality and happiness. I worried about my future. It's still ahead of me.

This scrap of paper I didn't burn. I filed it away as a future reminder of the trite but true fact that most of the things we worry about never come to pass. And the things which bring us genuine distress in time do pass and are obliterated in memory.

Perhaps it will remind me how senseless it is for the Christian to worry. Senseless, and, in a way, wicked. God cares for us. He invites us to cast our cares on him. The disorganized desk, the disorganized house are temporal and passing, and so are the things that keep us awake, for the most part. But the love of our Lord and his concern for us now and in the future are eternal.

Cast all your anxieties on him,
for he cares about you. I Peter 5:7

O Lord, who looks after our welfare, who knows our needs and our problems and shortcomings, Lord who gives us so much, give us the faith to trust in your love.

God Needs
No Memo Pad

A friend called to ask if I would chicken out on my promise to go rabbit hunting with him. I said I'd be happy to go rabbit hunting if I could finish the hunting season at my own house without shooting myself.

Each holiday season has its aftermath. For some it's overweight. Some have a budget bent out of shape. For me, it's the agony of trying to hunt the things I've squirreled away.

One year after Christmas I was asked to find some Very Important Papers. Very Important Papers are the very things I put in a very safe place. A place I then proceed to forget. It took me until the following Christmas to find them. They were in a drawer with the string of outdoor lights.

You'd think that would be a lesson, and it was. I put the papers in a very special place. Which I then proceeded to forget. The next time I received a call for them, I searched my entire filing cabinet without success. Well, not completely without success, because I found the recipe for cookies I'd been hunting for five years.

There was a happy ending to the story. In cleaning the top of my desk, I found the Very Important Papers in a file marked "Personal Correspondence." This time I delivered them quickly before I could lose them again.

All of this endless game of "Lost and Found" only serves to remind us of our human imperfections. We lose, we misplace, we forget.

Luckily for us, God needs no memo pad. We may think he forgets. We may think we have to send him a sharp notice.

"Now, look here, Lord. No doubt this has escaped your attention. . . ."

"May I remind you again. . . ."

"This is my final notice. . . ."

He doesn't need our reminders. He hasn't forgotten us or anything about us. Even the hairs of our head are numbered. Perhaps we should be thankful that he does forget one thing about us— our sins and our shortcomings.

While a master plan for our lives is serenely going on—literally over our heads—we are grubbing and grumbling and complicating our lives needlessly.

19

At least it's some consolation to know we're not alone in our failings.

My friend Betty called me long distance to ask if I'd written her a letter.

"I always save the best to read last," she said, "and I think I saved yours but apparently I lost it."

"That's all right," I said. "I just wrote to thank you for that marvelous memo calendar you sent me for next year. I know I'll find it very useful."

And I know I will—if only I can find it.

But even the hairs of your head are all numbered.
Matthew 10:30

Lord, help us to accept our shortcomings, the petty frustrations and abrasiveness of daily living. Help us to know that with all our forgetfulness, you will not forget us.

Mary on Good Friday

A mother's task is twofold. She is supposed to care for, to nurture, to protect. But she is also supposed to release, to relinquish, eventually to let go of her child. Her job is best done when she is no longer needed.

I heard a psychiatrist say that, and it started me to thinking how difficult it is for a mother to perform that second part of her duty. We need models in that major endeavor—the joy of letting go.

What was it like for Mary, I wonder . . . letting her Son go at such an early age? He was only 12 when he told her gravely and solemnly that he must be about his Father's business.

Did she feel like the mother who sends her son away to boarding school or college, out of the safe suburban neighborhood where he walked to school and where she knew his friends and their parents and grandparents? Once a child has gone away, even a little distance, he is in a different world, with different people, often with different ideas.

How did she feel, I wonder, when he became a wandering preacher? Like the mother whose son has taken a job in a far off country or joined the Peace Corps or a branch of military service?

He must have returned home with tales of dangers and perilous journeys and she must have said, as mothers do, "I'm glad I didn't know about it when it was happening. Now that you're safe at home, it's all right."

Not much is written about the mother Mary in the New Testament. A brash young man I know remarked one day that women have a minor part in all the recitals, and I retorted snappily that the accounts were written by men. I have a feeling that a woman writer might have covered Mary's activities more fully.

We do know that she accepted his growing maturity. At the feast of Cana she ordered the servants to do as he said. She respected his adulthood even though she was mystified by much that he did.

A Bible commentary I read observed, "She did not fully understand Jesus." What a poignant line. What mother ever does understand a son growing up and going away, especially one moving to a high destiny.

How did she feel on that day we now commemorate as Good Friday? Her son scourged, humiliated, killed by the fickle throngs which had hailed him with hosannas a short time before. Did she feel like the mother of an elected official who is a statesman one day and the target of editorial writers the next?

And how did she feel after his death? "A mother should never live longer than her child," a friend of mine said at the funeral of her beloved 46-year-old son. Even though she witnessed the ultimate glory, how Mary must have sorrowed. Was her grief like that of the mother whose son's life is lost in senseless battle? Was she bitter over the wasted years that might have been?

What was it like to be Mary? All mothers know a little, as we swell with pride and shrivel with worry and hurt, as we love and as we try to let our children go to the world. We know in our hearts.

Standing by the cross of Jesus [was] his mother . . .   John 19:25

Lord God, grant us grace to be parents, to love our children, and to express that love in its highest form—by letting go.

How To Be a Good Loser

Someone once said that the trouble with parenthood is that, by the time you're experienced, you're unemployable.

That is only too true. All of us who have children become experts, through painful on-the-job training. Just as we've learned how to handle the situation, the situation ceases to exist and something more challenging takes its place.

Even parents with large families find they can't use the knowledge gained from one child on the next. It's the same road with different bumps. As for the parent of an only child, she can do nothing but pass on her vast acquisition of wisdom to others.

One of the things I have learned is something the books on "the child from one to several" never teach you. That is, how to be a good loser. This is one of the things for which parents need to be trained.

When your children are very small, you begin playing games with them. When I was a child, it was dominoes, and when my son was 5 or 6, it was a game called Chutes and Ladders. Later on, he became interested in Monopoly, chess, checkers, and then athletic contests such as ping-pong.

In all of these games in which I was the chief opponent, it was my function to lose.

Now I'm sure there are parents and child guidance experts who would disagree with me. They believe in teaching a child the stern realities of life. When you compete against a more qualified opponent, you lose. As you become better qualified, you win. That is the way of the world.

I found it difficult to remember this when opposing a 5-year-old over the Chutes and Ladders board. I knew more ways than a riverboat gambler to palm the dice and slide down the chute so I'd come in second.

In chess and checkers, it wasn't so difficult. When a game involves skill rather than chance, it's easier to make a stupid play. When his father opposed him in baseball, it was amazing how often the regular hitter from our college team would strike out.

Ping-pong posed a problem for me. It's second nature to hit the ball back over the net. Sometimes from sheer ineptitude, I won. But after a year or two of ping-pong it dawned on me that I was play-ing my level best and still losing. I no longer had to pretend. I could go straight. A year or two later, the table tennis tables were turned. Sometimes my gallant teen-age opponent would throw the game to me.

Is such deception dishonest? If so, many a fond parent and grandparent is guilty. Perhaps it de-pends on the child. Some may need to be put down, others to be encouraged. And certainly all of us need to learn to lose gracefully, for such is the mark of maturity.

Perhaps we should be taught not to win, not just to "play the game," but to lose. For it is in losing that so often we win. It is in setting our hearts on coming in first, on being topdog, on being the winner that we end up, ultimately, as a loser.

Christ never stressed the value of winning, of coming in first, of lording it over others. He ex-pressed the beauty of humility, of sacrifice, and the victory to be gained in giving up. He gave his life for us.

He who loses his life for my sake will find it.

Matthew 10:39

Lord, forgive us our arrogance, our desire to win, to be first. Give us the love of Christ, that we may be willing to lose everything in service to you and to others.

The Beautiful Mother-in-Law

Mother comes off pretty well in the popular picture. A mother really has to work at it to slip from her pedestal.

With mother-in-law, it's another story. She's on the defensive before she begins. If she has a good relationship with daughter-in-law or even son-in-law, it's news. And nobody ever suggests dedicating a day to her. The French, I once read, treat her more kindly than most. Their name for mother-in-law is *belle mere*—beautiful mother—which is a slight concession.

Whenever I hear of tension between mother-in-law and daughter-in-law, I feel sad because I know it could be avoided. I know because of what happened between me and Aunt Lu.

I had no mother-in-law problem because my husband's mother died when he was a baby. Elsie, his youngish stepmother and I became friends and still are. He was almost through college and we were engaged when his mother's sister, Aunt Lu, looked him up. In a short time, I coined the phrase I used often: thank goodness she's not my mother-in-law.

27

Looking back, I can see that much of the difficulty arose because we were so much alike. Bossy. For instance, the first time she came to dinner, Aunt Lu wanted to show me how to make gravy because mine was lumpy. The nerve! As a bride I bristled. Nobody was going to come in my kitchen and make my gravy.

Because I believe in family ties, we kept up a formal relationship. Birthday cards, Christmas gifts, duty visits. But there was no real warmth. Luckily, Aunt Lu had another family. She had cared for the child of a working mother and when the girl grew up and the real mother died, Aunt Lu went to live with the girl and cared for her children.

Then everything fell apart. Aunt Lu was hospitalized with cancer. We visited her, and for the first time I felt a pang of pity for this tiny spunky woman as she sat up straight and assured us she "felt fine." Pity increased when we learned she'd lost her home. The family had broken up. They didn't want her back.

"Just find me a room some place," she told my husband. "Something I can afford on my pension."

"You can't do that," I said. "Bring her home with us."

"Are you crazy? You know you two don't get along."

"We'll get along," I said. "I'll see to it."

My husband compromised. He applied to a home

for the aged for which she was eligible. Temporarily she stayed with us. She was there on Thanksgiving Day. The turning point came when I looked at her, a woman who loved to cook, sitting on the sidelines on the feast day of the year. "Aunt Lu," I said impulsively. "Would you please make the gravy? Mine always gets so lumpy."

The end of the story is happy and sad. Happy because we became dear friends. She lived in the institution five years, valiantly fighting affliction, and we saw her often. She would visit us, baking her heavenly feathery rolls, having dinner ready when I came home from work. After 20 years of cooking, I was glad to have a helper in the kitchen. Amusingly, she became my protector against her cherished nephew, my husband.

"She works too hard," she'd scold him. "Let her rest."

The sad part came when she died. I wept over our loss, but more than that, over the lost years. If only we had moved together instead of drawing apart in the beginning, I could have had what every young wife needs—a *belle mere*.

Your daughter-in-law who loves you . . . is more to you than seven sons.   Ruth 4:15

Our Father God, bring love into our families, love for those who are closest to us and who so often see the worst instead of the best of us. Heal our hurts, smooth our frictions, let our homes mirror Christ's love for us.

29

The
Foolish
Wives

I know a young woman who is pretty and slim and shapely and young and bright and clever. She has a lovely home, three healthy children, and a husband who is quite successful at his job.

I often wonder why, in the face of all this, my young friend is so miserably unhappy. I do know some of the reasons because she tells us all at great length. Her successful young husband, on the way up, has not yet arrived sufficiently to give her full-time help, and she is tied down with the children she didn't want quite so close together. His job takes him out of town a great deal, and she is wistfully envious of his travels.

Even so, it saddens me to see her so actively antagonistic.

One evening she showed us slides of a trip they'd taken together. At least three times she used the phrase, "My stupid husband." Her stupid husband had bought the wrong kind of film, a projector that didn't work, and hadn't taken her to the right places at the right time.

I have another friend, an older one. Her children are grown and she has her husband all to herself. He isn't stupid. He's dull. She says so frankly, adding, "Sometimes I'm so bored, I could scream."

Perhaps I feel sympathy for these unsympathetic women because I see a little of myself and my earlier mistakes in them.

I remember being a young Army wife in an apartment with just my husband, far from home, and being "so bored I could scream." No job, no responsibilities, just long dull hours stretching endlessly ahead.

Now, as a widow with too many responsibilities, too much to do and no one to share the doing, I look back and think how foolish I was. What I wouldn't give now to be that young, slim me with a tiny apartment and a nice husband, alive and well.

It's human nature to wish for what we do not have. The grass is always greener on the other side of the fence. We rarely are sufficiently grateful for our blessings. We rarely know they are blessings until they are gone.

I wish I could say to all unhappy wives, "If you do not like your life in its present state, just wait a while. It will almost certainly change."

But you may not like the change.

There is a time for all things, a time to be tied down with family obligations and a time to be free of them. And for most women, there comes a time to be alone, often financially secure with no little ones underfoot, no husband messing up the house, no one, no one there.

Then, as in all the fairy tales and fables about wishes, you find what you wished for isn't what you wanted. What you really want is the time of your life that you wished away.

Love is patient and kind.   I Corinthians 13:4

Lord, help us to be grateful for the here and now. Teach us to count our blessings and to bless our loved ones. Forgive us for spending our precious days in idle daydreaming, and give us more of your love so we learn to care for one another and make each moment worthwhile.

Thank God for the Past and Live in the Present

It was a radio commercial for a savings company, and it based its message on a scene at a graduation ceremony.

"Time goes by so quickly," mused the mother in the dialog, as the father muttered something to himself about wishing he'd saved more money for college tuition.

Every now and then, as if carried on an echoing breeze, I can hear the wistful tone of the mother's voice, "Time goes by so quickly." How many other mothers think that every June.

Your friends tell you regularly that they can't believe in the passage of time.

"Your baby walking already? I can't believe it."

"Your son in school? I can't believe it."

"What! You say he's driving a car? He's six feet tall? He's graduating already?"

Sometimes you can't believe it yourself. I know I can't.

It seems like only yesterday that I delivered a not-quite-five-year-old to the kindergarten door, worrying whether or not he was sufficiently weather-proofed for the cold outside world. It was a closely guarded family secret that he could not yet tie his own shoes. We wondered if he'd flunk finger painting. Would he ever learn to read?

Time goes by so quickly. Next thing I knew, I was sitting in a car outside the big school.

The avalanche of third graders surged out as the 3:30 bell rang, and I would try to discern at a distance which plaid shirt and blue jeans covered my passenger.

A quick montage later and there was the same figure, only with longer legs and arms and a tremendous cello. We would fit cello and child and several friends into a very small car, often causing a double take among spectators when the cargo was unloaded.

Almost before I knew it, we were turning into another driveway, this one alongside the junior high school. And within a wink of an eye later, I was saying sadly to myself, "This is the last time I'll be driving to the junior high school."

Parents whose children are just beginning school

might find it hard to believe that parents whose children are ending will blink back tears, thinking, "No more PTA." It would have been hard for me to imagine back in those days when I was typing PTA stencils.

At last comes the beautiful blossoming time of new beginnings for young graduates. And as they surge forth in caps and gowns, we parents strain our eyes to find the familiar figure—just as we once looked for the little boy in blue jeans.

There is no way to recapture the past. It has gone by—and too quickly. But today is with us, a day in which we can "apply our hearts to wisdom"—and to appreciation of every golden moment. Thank God for the past and live in the present. He blessed us in the past, and he is with us today, too.

So teach us to number our days that we may get a heart of wisdom. Psalm 90:12

Heavenly Father, thank you for your blessings in my life. Keep me from living in the past, and help me look on each new day as a special gift. Strengthen me in the love of Christ to use the time of my life in service to others.

35

Father and
Our Father

To my knowledge, no one has ever written a sentimental ballad about fathers. There is no song beginning, "F is for the fives and tens he gave me."

Even though there is a Father's Day, dear to the hearts of advertisers and the manufacturers of shirts and neckties, those who keep a finger on the buying pulse will tell you that substantially less merchandise and fewer greeting cards are sold than are sold for Mother's Day.

Sometimes it seems as if fathers must be the greatest silent majority in the nation. A large percentage of the younger generation has no idea of what, "Life With Father," the all-powerful head of the household of another generation, is all about. Instead, today we have family togetherness, with some of the loudest expressions of opinion coming from the youngest members of the family. On television dramas and advertising commercials, the woman doesn't come off too bright, but father is the real boob on the tube.

Now, at our household it's different. We take good care of the father of the house, who is my father and is known as "Grandpa."

True, he is the silent minority especially when his ladyfriend—Grandpa is a widower—and I get to yakking away.

But we make efforts to include him in the conversation, such as saying, "Don't you think so?" and, "Are you listening?" or, "Why are you so quiet back there?"

We let him get lots of fresh air and exercise— walking the dogs, feeding them, watering them, chasing them to lock them up when we go away.

We always ask, "What would you like for dinner?" and sometimes even give it to him. We guard his health by making him eat salads and green vegetables, no matter how often he says, "No, thank you."

When our son was small, we let Grandpa have all the fun, taking the boy and sometimes three or four little friends to the baseball game. And hardly a Christmas goes by that we don't give him a new necktie.

And of course, if we can't think of a thing to get him for Father's Day and he has no hints to throw out except, "No more shirts," we have a secret weapon. We threaten to honor him as people do Mother on Mother's Day—by inviting all the relatives out and letting him do the cooking.

All that is in fun, of course. Seriously, we try to honor Father—Grandfather—because this is an earthly form of honoring "Our Father." It is right to do so. And when you love your father, it is easy to do.

Children, obey your parents in the Lord,
for this is right. Ephesians 6:1

God, we thank you for fathers who care for us on earth. Remind us that you are our heavenly Father, and bind us more closely to you in faith and love. Feed us with the grace of Jesus, your Son, that we may grow in love and respect for our fathers on earth and for you, our Father in heaven.

You're Making History Right Now

Whenever historic events are commemorated or famous phrases are quoted, I find myself wondering if the people being commemorated or quoted knew at the time that they were making history.

Most of the time they didn't. They simply did what they had to do at the moment and said what came into their minds, whether it was, "Nuts," or "Shoot if you must this old gray head." Even famous speeches like the Gettysburg Address were delivered to fulfill a commitment and often were received with apathy and none of the reverence they would one day command.

But it isn't only the famous speeches or great battles or stirring moments that are a part of our history. A speaker at a historical society meeting observed that there is much history in the lives of everyone, the everyday as well as the great.

"Most of us are not aware of it but we're making history today," she said.

Our grandparents didn't know they were making history when they traveled west across the plains or founded a city or started a fair, a ball, a picnic which became a time-honored tradition.

Grandmothers who served pumpkin pie, fathers who turned the old-fashioned ice cream freezer didn't know they were providing memories that would, in a sense, become history. But they were, and so are we all, all of the time.

When we do things with our family with any degree of continuity, it becomes a pattern which one day will be described as: "Our family always used to. . . ."

It's interesting to a parent how short the duration of "always" can be in a child's timetable. Three vacation trips to the same lake will become, "Our family always went camping in summer." A few years of a Fourth of July picnic will someday be the nostalgic, "We always had such fun on the Fourth of July."

Traditions and family history live on in many ways.

"Our family always celebrated Christmas the night before," one person will relate, while another will counter with, "Our family always celebrated early in the morning after church." And somehow the established tradition becomes the way to do it in another generation.

40

It's a sobering thought to reflect that mothers are making history when they bake cookies. Or welcome a new neighbor. Or perhaps when they fuss over trivialities. On the negative side we have, "My mother was always sick," and, "My father was always so busy, he never had any fun with us."

Sometimes we make history for others.

"I remember a family in our block," a man once said to me. "The mother was so warm and loving to the children. It was my first insight into what family life could be like. It wasn't that way at our house."

The next voice you hear may be your own and it may be remembered forever by the listener. It may go down in the annals of history for someone. And it may direct that little listener toward God or away from him.

Lord, thou hast been our dwelling place
in all generations.
Psalm 90:1

God, grant that the daily example we set, the daily remarks we make, the day by day history of our lives reflect your love, your teachings and your way.

A Clean Slate

Are you as good as you think you ought to be?

Probably not. Many of us think we fall far short of today's ideal morally and spiritually. According to some psychologists, a great many emotional problems of our time are caused by self-doubt and self-accusation. We just don't think we're nice people, and we know we should be better.

It's an idealistic age we're living in. We hear about our sick society and our shortcomings, but in many ways we set our sights higher. Other eras have had their heroes among the rich and powerful, the robber barons, the men who wrested a financial empire through ruthless means. Some generations have made heroes and heroines of those who flouted the moral code—the bootleggers, the gamblers, and the gold-digging blondes of the 1920s, for instance.

Today, in spite of the widely heralded spirit of revolt among the young, some of their heroes lead lives based on altruism: the medical missionaries, the volunteer workers. Many a businessman finds he's anything but a hero to his children, even though he pays the bills and provides a good living. Some young people want no part of a "money-grubbing society." As father tries to balance the budget and mother the checkbook, they feel out of step with their social-conscious teen-agers.

Some young people feel out of step with their own times. Tutoring youngsters in the inner city is the "in" thing to do in one church. The boy who'd rather spend Saturday morning tinkering with his car is made to feel selfish, and the girl who'd rather sew a new dress feels frivolous.

Parents sometimes feel out of step too. A home-owner has signed a petition at church saying he'd welcome persons of any skin coloring into his neighborhood, but then the new family moves in, and "For Sale" signs mushroom up and down the other front lawns. If all the houses are sold, he'll be in the minority group and suffer a possible financial loss. How to solve this sticky problem, a dilemma his grandfather never had to face?

What to do when our inner man—and woman—doesn't conform to what the outer being pretends to espouse in belief?

It helps to remember that we are only human. We can forgive our own weaknesses as we forgive those of others. We can, because Christ has forgiven us and forgives us each day.

And we can be grateful that every day brings a fresh new schedule of unsullied hours, a new slate on which we can write a new record of loving service.

Be kind to one another, tenderhearted, forgiving one another, as God in Christ forgave you.

Ephesians 4:32

God of mercy and understanding, you who see through our every weakness, make us aware of our shortcomings, but above all, aware of your gracious forgiveness through Jesus Christ.

Martha and
the Homemakers

"Have you sold your house yet?" my friend Max asked.

"No, not yet," I told him. "We're having a terrible time."

"What you should do," said Max, who is German-born and a Catholic, "is make a novena to St. Martha." (He pronounced it *Marta.*) "She helped my brother-in-law in California with his 28-family apartment when he'd almost given up on it."

I doubt that ecumenical give-and-take has advanced to the point where Protestants would ask the saints to intercede for them. But if ever I acquire a patron saint, I couldn't ask for a more appropriate one than Martha.

Of all the Biblical figures, she most commands my sympathy. I admire Paul tremendously, but I'm a little in awe of his strong character, and I have a feeling he wouldn't have approved of me at all. ("Woman, keep silence in the churches," I can hear him say.) But with Martha, I identify.

45

I've always had the feeling she wasn't treated quite fairly in the story involving her. If I recall correctly from the Sunday school version, Jesus was visiting in the home of Mary and Martha when Martha complained to him that she was doing all the work while Mary sat and listened to the conversation.

It happens in every family. There's one who enjoys the guests, and one who bustles about behind the scenes.

Jesus, rather than sympathizing, questioned her values.

"Martha, Martha, you are anxious and troubled about many things," he said, "but Mary has chosen the good portion." He meant listening to his words, and never has our Lord seemed more human.

Still I can't help feeling for Martha. After all, someone had to fix the dinner, and it wasn't fair that she should do all the work. True, we women tend to overemphasize the preparations sometimes to the detriment of our guest's comfort. The guest begins a fascinating story, and the eyes of the hostess glaze over as she tries to remember if she put the pickles in Grandma's cutglass dish.

We women do tend to place too much emphasis on home and things, and perhaps Jesus had this in mind when he chided Martha. After all, he set forth as a condition of Christianity, the willingness to forsake everything and follow him. This would be most difficult for the average home-loving home-maker to do.

Give up Grandma's cutglass pickle dish? And the marble-top washstand refinished with such loving care? And the ruffled curtains? And the rose garden at the back of our house? They are our security.

"The way I clean my refrigerator," a woman will say. We personalize and become possessive, even excluding husbandly rights.

Americans are especially materialistic and American women much possessed of their possessions. Home is where our heart is, and it's a rare woman who can say as men do, "What difference does it make who lives here after we sell the house?" Her house is part of her.

Even though we know we should, it's hard to put first things first when home is so dear. I'm sure Martha would understand.

One thing is needful. Mary has chosen the good portion, which shall not be taken away from her.

Luke 10:42

Lord, we homemakers are troubled about many material things. Forgive us our possessiveness and help us to see the true values in our lives and to place more worth in your words than in our worldly goods.

What's Wrong
with Middle Age?

"A middle-aged month is August/With its drowsy sounds of rest." Thus goes a line in a poem by Mary Joan Boyer. And it's true. August is a sun-ripened month, a little past its prime. The garden has lost the wonder and freshness of June, the full-blown glory of fruit and flower in July. The gardener who would have rushed out to view the first opening bud of a rose in May and tidily trimmed the hedge and pulled each offending weed now lolls back in the hammock.

"Ho-hum, another rose," is the attitude. "We've had a lot of roses this summer. Another weed? Well, no point in stooping down to pull it up. It'll die off in time."

The mating season is over in August. Birds, butterflies, and bees are preparing to leave the scene of their feasting and frolicking. As another poet, Sara Teasdale once wrote, we have reached the top of the hill; "the rest of the way will only be going down."

There's a sadness to it, yet should there be? Is middle age so bad? A visitor from Mars, reading our literature, hearing our songs, being trapped into an evening of television commercials might assume that it is a time to be dreaded.

American life is geared toward youth. We exalt it, bow down to it. Trim that bulge, fight that wrinkle, don't admit you remember way back when. Time is our enemy; the immature, our model.

A news magazine in a story on what it called "the command generation" described the real ruling class in the United States as one "cloaked in a conspiracy of silence . . . a generation that dares not, or prefers not, to speak its name—middle age."

While every psychedelic escapade of teen-agers and every anatomical twitch are headlined, and the halls of Congress ring with the medicares of the aged, the middle-aged are ignored. Yet this fifth of the nation, between the ages of 40 and 60, occupies the seats of power, makes the decisions, and pays the bills.

Despite its anonymity, middle age has compensations. One of them is in not being young. With tender amusement, a middle-aged mother may observe her teen-age daughter in an anguish brought on by such an earthshaking decision as what to wear, what if he doesn't ask me, what if he does, what to talk about? A facial blemish is a tragedy. A trivial *faux pas* is a fright to remember.

It is well for us to remember that there is a time for everything. A time to be young, a time to be old. And a wonderful time to be middle-aged, when the fullness of life is still there, but an occasional empty interlude does not cause the pain it once did. The August of life. When, if you're lucky, you have developed a philosophy, and, unless you're very unlucky or very ungrateful, you've discovered the basic truth—that in everything, even in middle age, God works for good.

We know that in everything God works for good with those who love him. Romans 8:28

Lord, lead us to accept maturity with grace and to give up our youth gracefully. Enable us to look back on our lives, to see where we've been and to look ahead to see where we're going, and to live each day with joy in Christ.

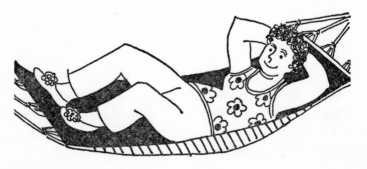

Let God
Mold Your Life

A friend of mine who learned to fly 25 years ago was telling me of the stern methods of his instructor in military flight training school. The instructor's regular name for the student was "stupid," despite the fact that the student performed somewhat better than the average. On one bad day, the instructor, overcome by the student's ineptitude, abandoned the speaking tube through which he usually shouted directions, hit his hands against the sides of the small training plane and then went into a perfect spin roll.

When the plane was right side up, the abashed student happened to glance down and notice that in his nervous state, he had neglected to fasten his seat belt. Had the spin roll not been so speedy and perfect, he might have had occasion to practice his parachute technique. For a minute, he felt as stupid as the teacher said he was.

"My head was really hanging low when I walked away from the plane that day," he recalled.

51

But there were better days. There was the day of the high wind when he was the only one, of teachers and students alike, to make a perfect landing. This time the instructor smiled broadly and congratulated him. The student muttered something like, "Aw, I should have done better."

"Do you think it was a good system?" I asked him, "being called stupid and given such rough treatment?"

"Yes, I do," he said promptly. "They're gentler on recruits today, and I don't think the system works as well. Hazing has all but disappeared from military academies, and hazing used to be pretty rough. But they didn't have cribbing and cheating then."

This is an interesting point, not only in the military but in every place where new, green recruits must be molded into professionals. The newcomer to a trade or profession was often the low man on the totem pole. When he had served a form of apprenticeship, he acquired dignity.

Then came the era of the manpower shortage when factories, plants, and offices were glad to get any warm body. Newcomers were welcomed no matter how inefficient.

How does it work—permissiveness with employees, students, children, trainees? Is it a better system, or was the school of hard knocks superior? We can find scriptural guidance to fit either belief— "Love one another," and also, "The Lord disciplines him whom he loves," or "chasteneth," to use the older word. And sometimes, we ruefully admit later, the chastening was needed, painful at the time but a blessing in disguise.

"Does the clay say to him who fashions it, 'What are you making?' " I love these words of Isaiah because I see myself so plainly in it, railing at the experienced hand, demanding my opinion in the molding even before I can see the ultimate design. Wanting to take shortcuts, not realizing certain basics must prevail.

One thing is for sure. The young man learning to fly an airplane today probably will be given gentler treatment than the one of a quarter century ago. But it would still be a good idea for him to remember to fasten his seat belt. The laws of discipline may be easier, but the law of gravity remains the same.

Does the clay say to him who fashions it, "What are you making?" Isaiah 45:9

Lord, strengthen us to believe in your ultimate wisdom as you fashion our lives, not always to our liking, not always in the mold or design we would have chosen, but to the ultimate good. Chasten us, as a kind father and teacher, fashion us into vessels to give glory to you.

The Almost Lost Art of Listening

I talked with a highly respected school principal in our community just before his retirement. He told me of former students who would come back to visit him.

"I always listen to them," he said. "The teacher can learn a lot from the students. If we've done nothing else at this school, we've stressed listening. It's almost become a lost art."

Listening is not only a nearly lost art, but in some circles it seems as painful to acquire as the skill of any other art.

I thought of a women's club meeting I attended one Christmas. The program consisted of half a dozen members reading brief seasonal stories, essays, verses. Not a long program. Not a dull or heavy one. Yet I was conscious of several members who seemed acutely uncomfortable to be sitting and listening.

One lighted cigarette after cigarette. Another wiggled and fidgeted, squirmed and turned like a puppy dog trying to find a comfortable spot. One apparently found it a waste of time to just listen and got out pins and curlers and put up her hair.

Having been on the other side of the program as a reader rather than listener, I know how distracting it was to each performer to look up at this perpetual motion and tried to make up for it by sitting absolutely motionless, eyes fixed on the speaker.

It's a test of skill but not an impossible one. You learn to perfect it if you make many platform appearances or have a husband in the public eye. You see others, eyes straying, fixed vacantly. You observe them stifling a yawn, buffing fingernails, wig-wagging to someone across the room, while the speaker is at his most eloquent, and you want to whisper shrilly, "Don't—we're watching you, too."

Wives listening to husbands and husbands listening to wives are great offenders. Maybe she's heard the funny story a dozen times or more. Maybe he's self-conscious that his wife is in the limelight. I once watched a minister whose wife was singing a solo and doing it beautifully; he buried his head in his hands as if listening were too painful to bear.

Perhaps listening could be taught at school. Sitting still is stressed only by the old-fashioned teacher today, but it has its place. "It's good muscle training," I used to tell wriggly Sunday school boys. "It will help you play baseball."

Much has been written about the "failure to communicate" between groups and generations. Most of it isn't the inability to talk as much as the inability to listen. No wonder we don't always hear our Lord when he calls or when he knocks at our door; we've lost the habit of listening. As the retiring principal said wisely, "The Lord gave us two ears but only one mouth. Maybe there was a reason."

Behold, I stand at the door and knock; if any one hears my voice and opens the door, I will come in to him and eat with him, and he with me.

Revelation 3:20

Lord, help us to listen—to one another, to those in trouble, to those who need us, but most of all, help us to listen for your voice and your knock at our door.

56

How's Your Image?

You wouldn't have to be a Rip Van Winkle awakened after a 20-year sleep to be out of touch with the language of today. Anyone who had been, literally, out of this world, for a few years, might have trouble with some of the popular phrases.

Take, for instance, the word, "image." It no longer calls to mind the Biblical connotation of the "image of God," or the "graven image." Nor does it mean what Grandpa meant when he said Junior was the "spittin' image" of his pop.

Image today means the character, the personality, the essence of an individual or, in our group-thinking world, more often the essence of a type or class of society. The image, whether it be of a person or product is something for which both advertisers and thought-control experts strive.

Often it's a shadowy thing created in the imagination of the inventor and substantiated by preselected evidence. And it may bear little resemblance to reality.

Is the image presented that of the housewife and mother? We all know what her popular image is today. She's unhappy with her role in life, a trapped prisoner of her home, brooding over her unrealized potential.

Are her children grown so she can enjoy a degree of freedom? Now she's a clubwoman, a Helen Hokinson type, one of "The Girls," frittering away time at busy work.

Is she older? She's a victim of the "empty nest syndrome." The children have gone. They don't come back because she was such a smothering "Mom." (Mothers come off badly in the imagery field today.) She's driving her husband to his grave by her demands.

Is the image presented the man of the house? He's a Dagwood, the father who never knows best and is constantly being outwitted by his clever wife and scheming children. The children? They're over-organized and pressured. The teen-agers? Rebels in baggy clothes and long hair.

The trouble is that some people fit these pat patterns, but many do not. There are women who love domesticity, do good works, and stay sound and smiling into old age. There are men who really are the head of the house, children organized and disorganized, and teen-agers who are nice kids.

How's your image? More important, how's your acceptance of the images you see on your television screen, in the paperbacks, in the news headlines? Do you take them at face value and say, "Yes, that group, that race, that country is like that." Or do you question, look to the individual, the substance rather than the shadow? Do you say with Christopher Morley's heroine, Kitty Foyle, "Every time I find myself thinking something, I stop and ask, who was it figured it out that I was supposed to think that way?"

Perhaps we should formulate our own ideas about the image of others, and our own independent image, too. Better still, we might go back to an older use of the word—and try to remember that God created us in his image.

You have put off the old nature . . . which is being renewed in knowledge after the image of its creator. Colossians 3:10

God, do not let us take the words of the world at face value. Remind us to question and compare and assess, not by worldly standards but by the life Christ has lived for us.

The Richness
of Old Age

I was driving home one lovely September day, noticing with pleasure the burnished leaves of the maples and the golden oaks and the scarlet sumac along the road. A warm and happy feeling enveloped me, and I stopped to analyze it. I had just come from an old folks home and visiting there had given me such a pleasant glow, something akin to the emotions aroused by warm sunshine and autumn colors.

The home is called an old folks' home, in honest and old-fashioned terminology, not a senior citizens' villa or geriatrics center or retirement community. Just an old folks home, but the people who lived there—predominantly women, as is usually the case—were busy and cheerful.

They were getting ready for a forthcoming fair, given annually. All year long they sew and do handicrafts and make things to sell, and each per-

60

son keeps the money his or her handiwork brings. There's a tea for board members along with the fair, and some of the men gardeners were grooming their prize dahlias for the table decorations.

It was nothing like the grim picture of old age often drawn for us today. It occurred to me that later years are dreaded unnecessarily. As Maurice Chevalier once said, "Old age isn't so bad when you consider the alternative."

But the truth is that old age isn't all that bad. It's out of style, of course. In many new suburbs, you rarely see an old person—only young couples and their young families. The three level family— grandparents, parents, children—somehow doesn't go with the split-level civilization.

Probably I'm prejudiced because for many years we had a three-level family, and it seemed to work out pretty well. It began when my parents came to live with me when my husband went into service during World War II, and I was alone in a new home. They stayed on, and then our son was born and I needed someone to look after him when I went back to work, and built-in baby sitters were nice to have.

But more than that, it seemed to us that it was good to have three generations together. Not perfect—no family is. But we felt the advantages outweighed the drawbacks.

My mother was marvelously active and vigorous for many years, and then gradually she became senile. Many families would have felt it necessary —and with good cause—to put her in a home. We didn't and it created problems. Second childhood is just that, a state becoming more and more like infancy. There are diapers and hand feeding and now and then the granny or grandpa runs away and gets lost.

Patience is not my long suit, but it helped to remember, and remind our son, that in infancy we all are fed and cleaned. Bathing and caring for our vacant-eyed little granny was sometimes a chore but also service for someone you loved.

When she died, it was like a dried leaf blowing from a branch, and the family tree was bare without it. But we had enjoyed her warm and glowing autumn years, and I will always think our family life was the richer for it.

Even to your old age I am he, and to gray hairs I will carry you.

Isaiah 46:4

Heavenly Father, ours is a world geared to youth today and often we ignore the elderly and the problems of aging. Make us aware, not of the duty but of the privilege of caring for our seniors, as Christ cares for all of us.

The Pleasure
of Your Own
Company

"I guess I'm peculiar," the little old lady said apologetically, "but I enjoy my own company."

This is a damaging admission in our present-day society. The pleasure of your own company is something to be avoided. The "truly integrated personality" is supposed to "act in conformity" with his "peer group."

The problem of this little old lady, who happens to be 80, is that she doesn't want to live with others of her peer group, other little old ladies in a senior citizens' home or even one of the many manors where she'd have her own apartment and join the others in the dining room or lounge or therapy workshop.

She wants to stay on in her own old house. She wants to live alone. Not in an institution, not with her children, not even with a friend. Just by herself. And it's causing others to look at her askance.

Ours is a group society from nursery preschool to the planned community for retired couples. It's geared to the group, and the person who wants to be solitary now and then is suspect. When a criminal is apprehended, it's a part of the pattern for someone who knew him in his youth to recall him as being a "loner." They just knew he wouldn't turn out well.

We tend to forget the lone eagle and the tall figures of history who didn't fit in because they stood out.

If young Tom Edison were a boy today, he'd be discouraged from puttering around alone in a laboratory and would be put to work in the group project at the boys' club. As for Thoreau, he'd be pressured into joining a garden club or at least the bird watchers' society in self-defense.

Group living starts with the littlest ones. The solemn written appraisal sent home from nursery school is concerned not only with the learning of new skills but with how well the child gets along with others.

In the teens, it's taken for granted that all boys and girls are a part of an organization. Should a boy avoid Teen Town, come home, and go to his room and read a book, his mother starts worrying. Maybe he needs group therapy.

Even the housewife is encouraged to join a gym class, participate in church work, or be active in politics to get her out of the house. If she rather enjoys the silence of home without even a voice from a box to shatter her thoughts, she hides the fact.

No man is an island, of course, and antisocial people do sometimes commit antisocial acts. Civilization means the mastery of getting along with others, sharing and cooperating. But, on the other hand, God's great gift to us is our own unique personality and being. Life lived solely with others can concern itself with superficials and never delve into the depths which are in our own soul. Fortunate is the person who can enjoy being alone—with God. But it takes practice. As the little old lady reminded us cheerfully, "If you want to enjoy your own company when you're 80, you'd better practice when you're 8."

Jesus went up into the hills by himself to pray. When evening came, he was there alone.
Matthew 14:23

Lord, help us to enjoy your great gift to us—ourselves—and to spend a part of each day alone in communion with you.

Patience
with Youth

October is birthday month in our family. It's a pretty good month for that sort of thing. For at least the first 10 years of our son's life, we had an outdoor party annually, and never once were we rained out—or in. You can hardly beat that.

We went from pony rides to wiener roasts to cave exploring to airplane rides, as one interest gave way to another. One year we spent the birthday afternoon—again a bright, blue, beautiful day—at drivers' license headquarters. It was the 16th birthday.

Sixteen is a magical mystical time for a youngster, the growing up year, but it's also a year of frustration for parents.

"Sixteen isn't an age; it's a disease," said one exasperated father.

As one who was encountering the standard experiences of teen-age rebellion and assertiveness and parental despair, it was a great relief for me to lunch with a friend one day and unburden myself. She has three sons and has some perspective to draw on.

"Oh 16," she said with a laugh. "That was an awful year."

It was her eldest, she recalled, who was the worst problem at that age.

"He was surly, insolent, insulting," she related. "Once when I was trying to get a family group picture, I asked them all to smile and just as I snapped the shutter, he stuck his tongue out. We still have that picture in the album.

"Most of the time, he challenged everything I said," she continued. "I remembered once we were driving on a vacation, and I innocently made the remark—chattering as I do—that I felt sorry for truck drivers. They must have a hard life. Well, he took it up for debate and argued with me for an hour until I was reduced to tears. It was that way with everything.

"I kept saying, if only we hadn't sent him to church camp. We sent him away the summer he was 16, hoping he'd come back, wanting to be a minister or missionary. Instead, he came back from camp and said to his younger brothers, 'I learned one thing at camp. We don't have to do everything mom and dad tell us to do.'

"Nothing we ever did was right. And he never did a thing if he sensed we wanted him to do it."

Where is this juvenile terror now? He's a paragon of young manhood, successful professionally, well adjusted socially, and writes regular, solicitous loving letters to his parents. His two younger brothers who gave their parents similar 16-year-old pains turned out equally well.

For those who have gone through these agonies or are beginning them, my experienced friend had words of wisdom.

"My father used to say that bringing up a boy is like going fishing," she said. "When the fish is pulling and tugging at the line, you should relax and let him have his way. Then when he relaxes, you can pull him in."

And you both relax a little more after age 16.

The farmer waits for the precious fruit of the earth, being patient over it until it receives the early and the late rain. You also be patient. James 5:7

God, give us patience with our rebellious young, even as you have patience with us. Help us see them as reflections of ourselves, when we arrogantly demand, "Now look here, Lord," and want to have our way in all things. Enable us to deal with them as Christ taught us—with love.

Politicians and Citizens

Election year is the time for all good men to come to the aid of their party.

It is also the time for extravagant claims and charges, a time of excesses and bitterness and rash remarks. There is mounting tension, like an elastic band stretched taut, near to snapping. Best friends are cool to one another and families verge on feuding.

Then it is all over. The hoopla, the shouting, the sweet victory, and the disappointing defeat. After election week, the rancor will depart, temperatures will simmer down. And after a very short while, many of the people who voted for the man who won become disenchanted and start planning for his defeat.

It's a great game, politics, and it's a pity that the main event occurs only every four years. For some

—the hard core group—it's a full-time profession, and they can smile with amusement at the rest of us because they know how little influence the election-year politician has on the big business of government.

He's like the Christian who goes to church on Christmas and Easter. He feels self-righteous, but he doesn't have much effect on planning, policy, or budget.

The election-year politico doesn't think so. He views himself—often it's herself—as a good citizen, and it's interesting to see how often the name "citizen" is used in election years. The "Citizens for Good Government" tag sounds impressive.

The election year citizen will tell you that he's for the man not the party; and if he's really enthusiastic, he'll give him the highest praise possible —he'll say he isn't "really a politician."

My husband, who held political office and was born into a political family, once received a letter from a woman who thought she was complimenting him for his stand on a certain issue.

"If it weren't for men like you," she wrote, "our state would be in the hands of the politicians."

My husband, who had worked his way up from precinct level, was halfway between amusement and sadness.

"What in the world does she think I am?" he asked.

We met many politicians, some good, some unscrupulous but a surprising number of them dedicated, honest, sincere. They had respect for one another, regardless of party, and a kind of fellow feeling of camaraderie, like men who had fought in the same war—even on opposite sides—and knew the glory and the false glory.

People who stand on the fringe miss a lot. I can't feel that Christ's admonition to, "Render unto Caesar" meant simply to pay your taxes and take no further interest in the government. For he was in the thick of things, taking sides on issues, taking a stand, working for change.

Those who like the "ins" and those who prefer the "outs" both have a job to do.

Render therefore to Caesar the things that are Caesar's, and to God the things that are God's.

Matthew 22:21

God, direct our interests and activities toward helping to shape just government for all citizens.

71

Be Thankful for Differences

There's a religious group for teen-agers in our suburb which has become tremendously successful. Its popularity has aroused amazement—and perhaps a little envy—on the part of others who have tried to reach and teach this often callous and disinterested group of young people.

"I understand it's pretty far to the left," one critic said to me. "A bunch of wild-eyed liberals run it."

"I hear it's a hotbed of conservatism," said someone else. "A regular junior John Birch society."

Curious as to how one group could fit both descriptions, I slipped into a meeting one night. I found it to be very much like the church league sessions I remembered from my teens. They sang songs. They laughed over memories of an outing they'd been on and planned another one. And an earnest young man held their rapt attention as he told them about Jesus Christ.

I can see where those rumors got started though. Some of the teachings of Christ are "way out there." And anyone who tells stories from the Bible may be called that awful thing, a "fundamentalist."

I don't know how other church lay people feel, but I for one get a little tired of all this name calling, from left to right and vice versa. It seems a great waste of good Christian energy.

The names themselves are subject to dispute. To some, a "liberal" is a courageous idealist, while to others, he's an unshaven radical who wants to overthrow the government and probably smokes marijuana. A "conservative" is a sound and sensible person to some—or a stuffy, pompous person with a turn-of-the-century high collar and views to match.

In church life, a liberal is suspected of wanting to introduce go-go girls to the Sunday morning ritual. And a conservative is looked on as interested only in the contents of the collection plate to build a new air-conditioned addition to the building.

Methodist Bishop Gerald Kennedy of Los Angeles once suggested that "instead of merely putting up with somebody who is different than we are, let

73

us thank God that he gives us an authentic witness from the other side of the hill."

As a liberal, said Bishop Kennedy, he is grateful to the fundamentalists for their "emphasis on the unchanging and eternal verities of our faith." He said fundamentalists in turn might respect the Christian motivation of liberals who "feel so strongly about the relevancy of the church that they want to find ways to make it speak to the modern world."

As one frequently caught in the middle, I think we might be thankful for these varied accents as a sign of vigor and youth in our church life of today. Be thankful for "left," be thankful for the right. And be thankful that we have a center that brings us together—Jesus Christ, the Mediator who unites us in him.

Judge not, and you will not be judged; condemn not, and you will not be condemned; forgive, and you will be forgiven.

Luke 6:37

Lord, grant us that great virtue of tolerance. Help us not only to understand but to be grateful for those whose views are different, remembering that Christ did not judge or condemn, but forgave.

The Wishbone

I was deboning a chicken to make a special dish for a luncheon I was hosting. Suddenly, without any effort on my part, a wishbone fell out, clean and intact.

I stood looking at it for a moment, wondering what to do with it. There's not much you can do with a wishbone when you live alone. It takes two to tangle over which one will break off the longer piece of bone and thus get his wish, as popular folklore has it. It's a test of skill or strength or luck, but at any rate, it's competitive, and you can't very well compete against yourself.

As I reflected on this fact, I found myself remembering other years and how exciting a thing the wishbone was. For one thing, you didn't have chicken or turkey for dinner just any day of the week. In our modest circumstances, you didn't even have chicken every Sunday. Chicken or turkey was for grand occasions, like Thanksgiving, and it meant a celebration.

One of the moments of tension was the uncovering of the wishbone. Would it break accidentally or come out intact? If intact, it was carefully hung up to dry until the time came to "make a wish."

Usually it was my mother and I who made the wishes. Looking back, I realize that she let me manipulate the forked breastbone so I'd bend it over and break the longer piece and win. In later years, I tried to let her win, knowing that her wish would be for me and something more than I could wish for myself.

What would I wish for now, if I were still to believe in the magic of the wishbone and had a partner at the other end? Would I wish for peace for the world? Hardly, knowing that peace is something to work for, something to pray for, but hardly a subject of chance for a wisp of a wish.

Happiness for one's child? This is something every mother wishes, yet knows in her heart is both unattainable and undesirable. It takes a leavening amount of unhappiness to form character and integrity, and continuous happiness isn't as enviable a state as the young might think.

Would I wish for something tangible, like money? A comfortable retirement? Good health? The wish my mother used to tease me about—"a nice young man with rosy cheeks?" Unfortunately, by the time you make serious wishes, you also know wishing won't make it so.

Nothing to wish for—a sad state of affairs. Is it maturity? or only old age? Or is it wisdom—to know that food and drink and temporal happiness is less important than the intangibles of peace and joy in the Spirit?

There are all kinds of artsy-craftsy things the talented can make with wishbones nowadays but I have neither nimble fingers nor storage space. Finally—with some nostalgic regret—I threw the wishbone away, still intact, hoping that somewhere, boys and girls making wishes might have them all come true. For myself, I only hoped—not wished —that the chicken dish for my guests would be a success.

The kingdom of God does not mean food and drink but righteousness and peace and joy in the Holy Spirit. Romans 14:17

Lord, we know how futile wishing is and how few things are really worth the heartfelt wishing. Give us the wisdom to know the difference and the courage to work instead of wish.

77

Thoughts for a Thankful Heart

Is it hard for you to feel thankful? Let me offer for your consideration this fragment of conversation that drifted by as I was hurrying through a downtown department store one noon hour.

"How's your son?" asked a disembodied feminine voice.

"We don't know yet," a man's voice replied. "They're taking the bandages off this afternoon."

That was all, but it was enough to start me thinking. Maybe you will ponder on it, too. Maybe it will push some of your problems into the background . . . those vexations about home appliances and matching swatches of fabric and planning menus and dealing with abrasive personalities and first it's one thing and then another in the life of an average wife and mother.

How's your son?

Sleeping peacefully in his crib? Blowing bubbles as he sits in his high chair? Spooning spinach onto the carpet? Making a mess out of the dresser drawer?

How's your son? Or your daughter?

Goofing off, as usual? Rushing to a date leaving a bed unmade, a room looking as if a cyclone had struck it?

Fighting with little brother or sister? Teasing the cat? Watching television and don't you let me hear you complain you have homework to do at nine o'clock tonight. . . .

Playing the electric guitar with the amplifier that is going to drive you stark raving mad. . . .

Hanging on the telephone and if you don't stop that silly giggling this very minute. . . .

How's your son? How's the son of your friend or neighbor or the woman who comes to work for you on Tuesdays?

"We don't know . . . he's in the Army . . . he's in another country . . . he ran away . . . the last time we heard from him, he was on the West Coast. . . ."

"He's under oxygen . . . they'll operate tomorrow . . . they're taking the bandages off this afternoon."

How's your son? If your answer is a simple, prosaic statement of fact or an expression of exasperation or annoyance or motherly resignation, be thankful. Thank God. Thank his Son.

How's your son? And your daughter? And husband? And parents? How are you? And how's your thankful heart?

O give thanks to the Lord, for he is good; for his steadfast love endures forever.

Psalm 106:1

O God, we know in our hearts how thankful we should be for the many blessings of life. Help us to see the blessings in our own lives. Give us thankful hearts.

The Echo from the Woods

"This has been the most marvelous flight," I told the airline steward. "You crew members have really outdone yourselves. I don't know when I've had such marvelous service."

The young man smiled.

"We have a German saying," he replied, "that when you cry into the woods, the echo comes back. We find on these flights that when our passengers are in a happy mood, it echoes back to us and we in turn are nicer to them, and then that good feeling comes back, too."

This capsule lesson in human relations is something most parents know and the results are what we try to achieve. We do our best to send out positive thoughts, hoping they'll be echoed back by our children. Sometimes we wonder if we're merely talking to the trees or crying to the wind.

But then again, the echo comes back with startling clarity.

There was a boy who moved from a grade school that was mildly integrated to a junior high that was completely integrated. He was uneasy and told his mother he was.

"The class I hate most is gym," he said. "They're mostly black kids and not a bit friendly. They don't like me."

"Maybe they think you don't like them," his mother said, "so they're reacting first."

"Have you thought of saying something nice?" she went on. "Not something insincere but true. Like, 'Say, you're good at that. I wish I could do as well as you.' It's hard to dislike someone who praises you."

Weeks went by. The mother was driving her son across town one day when he waved to a black boy on a street corner.

"Friend of mine from school," he explained. "Gym class." Then he went on, "You know, they're not hard to get to know. If you're nice to them. You say something like, 'Say, you're good at that game. I wish I could do that well.' And they're real friendly."

His mother shot him a sharp look, wondering if he were kidding. But he was earnest and serious about his own new theory.

Sometimes a religious parent tries and tries to get through, but his ideas seem to fall on deaf ears.

"I keep telling my son prayer can help when you're under tension," I said to a father, "but I don't seem to get across."

"Maybe you do more than you know," he replied. "I used to tell my son the same thing with no results. Then one day, he said, 'You know I tried something you're always preaching and it worked.' It seemed he'd been on his way back to college when a terrific rain came down. He stopped on a lonely country road. When he tried to start again, the car wouldn't budge. Over and over, he tried the ignition. Nothing happened. He started to panic.

"Then I remembered what you always said," he told his father later, "so I sat quietly and prayed for a few minutes. And when I tried to start the car again, what do you know? It started."

"I have a feeling the engine was flooded," the father said with a grin, "and the waiting was all that was needed. But who knows?"

Who indeed? There are all sorts of ways of crying into the woods. Sometimes it's an echo that comes back. And sometimes an answer.

Train up a child in the way he should go, and when he is old he will not depart from it.

Proverbs 22:6

Lord, so often we cry out with shrill, strident voices and never pause to listen. When we cry despair, it is despair that is echoed back. Help us to sing out in faith, so that the echo from the woods brings blessed reassurance back to us.

Suppose You Could Do It All Over

"I wish life were like duplicate bridge," a friend said. "You know—where the same hand is played in two different ways. You can't help wondering how your life would have turned out if you had played your hand just a little differently at some key points."

"Not that I'm dissatisfied with the way mine has turned out," she added hastily. "But lately I found myself thinking about one of those key decisions. It was during World War II before I was married. I had an interesting job and my boss was transferred to Texas. He wanted me to go along but I decided against it. I've often wondered what would have happened if I'd taken that job. I wouldn't have the same husband, the same children, the same kind of home."

Most of us can look back on similar forks in the road. We took one of two paths that stretched ahead and, as the Robert Frost poem puts it, "that has made all the difference."

My mother once told me that her mother had planned a trip to California for her. Grandmother thought mother was getting too serious with a certain ardent suitor.

"I'm going to write your uncle in California tomorrow," she said.

They were her last words. She died that night. The trip was never taken, and mother married the young man who became my father.

The last night of my freshman year in college, I was asked for a date by two boys I'd been going with, off and on.

I accepted one and turned down the other. Neither had been an especially romantic attachment at the time but five years later I married the student with whom I had the date. The other one—as always happened—went on to fame and fortune. He never married, though I don't believe he suffered from a broken heart.

Even so, you can't help pondering those minor decisions that led to major developments. The party you didn't want to attend—where you met someone who played an important part in your future.

What if you could take the original hand and play it over? Would you use your trump cards in quite the same way? Would you discard the same ones at the same time?

Then there's another point. Would you have the courage to play the hand altogether differently? What if it turned out to be disastrous? What if you gambled for a grand slam and went set?

Luckily for us, the mistakes we made aren't eternally irrevocable. God overlooks our poor plays, forgives our mistakes, and often in looking back, we can say where his hand took failure on our part and remade it into success.

Few of us would want to change our lives drastically. Even the friend who wonders what kind of life she would have had in Texas wouldn't trade her two children for the LBJ ranch.

There are exceptions, of course. Another woman, asked if she'd like to play her hand of life over again, said she certainly would.

"Only this time," she said. "I'd call for a new deal."

Walk in love, as Christ loved us and gave himself up for us. Ephesians 5:2

Lord of compassion and wisdom and understanding, remind us that we cannot play our hands over in the game of life or erase our mistakes. Strengthen us in the forgiveness and mercy you have shown us Jesus Christ that we may walk in his love.

Christmas
Is...

Christmas is happiness and happiness is Christmas.

Christmas is Jesus' birthday, as the little children sing about it, and, from older voices, it is a silent night and a holy night, bringing joy to the world.

Christmas is fun and frolic and festivity. It is all the tradition of treasured things "our family has always" done, as well as the traditions remembered from other days. It is the heritage of generations, the fruitcake from a recipe written in spidery handwriting on yellowed paper, the ornament brought from another country in an immigrant's trunk, the story told in another tongue.

Christmas is family and room for the family. It is a baby in the manger, in a cradle, in a crib, in a playpen, in a plastic armrest. It is man reborn annually with spirit and good intentions reborn. It is parents whispering secrets and staying up late to assemble gifts and wrap presents.

It is family from far away. Young men and women home from college and reunions and catching up with the news and reliving all the memories of Christmases past. Sometimes Christmas is loneliness and, on the part of the aware, a heightened consciousness of loneliness and separateness in others.

Christmas is giving and receiving. It is the package you tied clumsily for your mother many years ago. It is the year of your first skates and best doll and candy from your first boy friend.

Christmas is reverence. It is religion. It is church. Worship services at midnight. Worship services in the early dawn. Worship services at bright midday. Worship services at home. The violet and pink candles in the Advent wreath.

Christmas is music. Deep throated organ music. Voices in chorus. Sleigh bells ringing. A music box with a tinkling measured melody.

Christmas is light. Shopping center lights blazing. Strings of lights scalloping the suburbs. Christmas tree lights that bubble and wink and twinkle and burn out and must be checked and replaced because darkness is alien to Christmas. It is candlelight in the window for the carolers. It is light for the world.

Christmas is anti-war, anti-rebellion, anti-hate.

It is cease-fire and reconciliation and forgiveness of others as we would be forgiven, and the sound of chimes drowning out the harsh noises of the busy world.

Christmas is peace on earth, good will toward men and peace on earth to men of good will and the same message in many translations.

Christmas is the hope of everlasting peace.

Christmas is Christ in the world.

To you is born this day in the city of David a Savior, who is Christ the Lord. Luke 2:11

God our Father, who sent us God the Son, keep our hearts mindful of the true meaning of Christmas, the real cause for happiness, the most precious gift. Amid the tinsel and the glitter and the clamor and noise, keep us aware of Christ and let our love reflect his everlasting love.

89

Not Every
Christmas Is
a Merry One

A friend came out to dinner the night before her birthday and stayed overnight. As I prepared breakfast the next morning, it occurred to me that a festive touch was in order. I didn't have a fancy coffee cake, just the routine bacon, eggs, and toast, so I put a birthday candle in the center of her grapefruit half.

"It's a birthday cake for dieters," I explained when she came to the table.

"Well, I guess you make your own birthday," she said with a laugh. "I saw a book with a title like that—*Make Your Own Christmas*. Of course, it referred to making things with your hands for Christmas, but it's true in the broader sense, too. You make your own holidays regardless of circumstances."

There's sense in this. Not every Christmas is a merry one for everyone. There are the Christmases of your childhood, the ones out of a storybook with the house filled with the fragrance of pine and spruce and spice and with rustly paper, bulky packages, whispered conferences.

There are the college vacation Christmases with parties and a laugh a minute. There's the Christmas when you've just fallen in love and walk arm in arm through the first snowfall, and the bells are ringing just for you.

There's Christmas for newlyweds, the first tree, the first turkey dinner for relatives, the first decorations for the new home.

Then there are the other kinds of Christmas.

The Christmas when the most important person of all is half a world away, and you mail the packages the first of December and wish you could go to sleep and not wake up until well into the new year.

The first Christmas after someone has died and you find the card in that dear familiar handwriting, accidentally tucked away with last year's leftover wrappings. And you try to go through the motions and put up the same ornaments and with every one there's a memory.

There may be a Christmas you spend in a hospital or in a nursing home or all alone in a strange place. Christmas Eve in an airport, Christmas dinner in a restaurant, a Christmas that is "just another day."

No matter where or how or what the circumstances, you can make Christmas the day it should be. Not necessarily a festive feast day, but the observance of a great moment in Christian history. Above all other days, it's the one when you should not feel lonely even if you are alone, the day when you should light the candle rather than curse your own dark fortune.

It may not be your greatest memory of Christmas. Maybe next year will be better, so happy that you'll look back on the sad one and regret that you didn't make more of it.

You can make your own Christmas because Christmas isn't something out there, spelled out in lights, dancing in tinsel.

It's within, waiting to come out, in its original untinseled, untarnished form.

And with it is the knowledge that God gives us dark days, gives us our share of suffering, but he also gave us his Son that we might have Christmas every year of our lives and life everlasting.

We rejoice in our sufferings, knowing that suffering produces endurance, and endurance produces character, and character produces hope.

Romans 5:3-4

Lord, give us strength to endure the days that are not the happy ones, and give us the sensitivity to reach out to those around us, the sorrowing and the sad and the lonely, and warm their lives with the real spirit of Christmas.

The Sweet Life— Fact or Fiction

It was an old movie, quite old, about seven years old. But that's not terribly old for television and it was new to me because I don't see many movies.

This one, I admitted with a laugh to friends with whom we dined, was not exactly recommended for family viewing. It was an Italian film about decadence among the idle rich. Its title, translated, meant "the sweet life."

A friend at the dinner told me a church group had been bombarding the television station with calls all day, imploring them not to show the film. After I saw it, I wondered if they were performing a service. Perhaps everyone in the formative years should be encouraged to see such a film because never have the wages of sin been painted in more shabby and shoddy tones.

Our teen-ager watched it five minutes and found it too boring. A middle-aged house guest stuck it out half an hour, then pleaded fatigue. I don't like unfinished plots so I stayed with it until 1:30 A.M.

It was a sad picture, about people with too much money and nothing to do but indulge in the flesh-pots of sex and alcohol. This is the sweet life? It made the pursuit of pleasure look oppressively dull. Honest work and clean living seemed joyous by contrast.

I couldn't help thinking how different is the concept of the sweet life to many of us fortunate enough to have to struggle for financial survival. The family trying to get the kid's teeth straightened, the college tuition paid, the mortgage on the house lifted before the walls fall in.

I thought of the daily routine in the average household. Husband and wife having breakfast together, getting children off to school and to music lessons and church and meetings. Picnics in the summer and vacation camping trips and holidays.

I thought of vegetables fresh from the garden and home canned fruits and peach preserves bubbling on the stove. I thought of small towns all over America where home comings are celebrated and centennials where men grow beards, and antiquers try to make the pump organ work for a special service, and drum majorettes prance, and merchants deck floats with crepe paper, and softball teams play under the lights in the park, and couples sit on benches and hold hands and plan the kind of life they'll lead.

I thought of families living in Christ and professing his name and trying to live in his way. Of lives dedicated to helping others rather than to pleasure and self-indulgence.

The sweet life. This is the real sweet life. Even the Monday morning alarm clock sounds good. Except maybe when you've stayed up too late on Sunday night watching a not very good movie.

Walk by the Spirit, and do not gratify the desires of the flesh.

Galatians 5:16

God, grant us perspective, give us discrimination to determine the true sweets of life, a life, not of self but of others, a life in Christ.

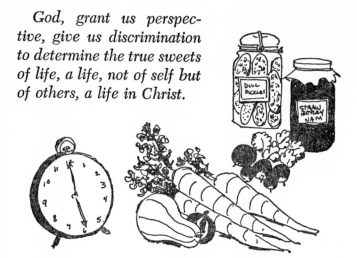

Is It a
Rotten World?

The teen-ager had just come home from the movies and was sitting in the kitchen, fortifying himself with half an apple pie.

"How was the movie? Was it good?" I asked.

"Oh—not really." The favorite teen-age form of faint criticism. "It was all about what a rotten world we live in."

The plot of the movie, drawn out between bites of pie, turned out to be about the intolerance of one group for another, intolerance so bitter that it culminated in mass murder. Related in skeleton form, it sounded like thinly veiled propaganda of one point of view and highly unlikely "realism." But it started me thinking and kept me thinking for some time.

"What a rotten world we live in."

This seems to be the subtitle of many of the movies, plays, and books. The romantic boy-meets-girl musicals have given way to clinical studies of perversion. Man's inhumanity to man is a pervading theme. The only time you see a happy ending is on the late late show.

"I've seen some of the movies you used to see. They're on television now," a boy told his mother. "Real fairy tales. How did you ever swallow that stuff?"

"Maybe so," said his mother, "but at least we knew we were watching fantasy.

"When we came back to our own lives, it was coming back to the world of reality. Now you believe you're seeing reality on the screen but what do you think when you come back to your own lives which are so different? Does it make your life seem unreal?"

"A slice of life" they used to call dramas of stark realism which showed the tawdry, the seamy, the sordid side.

A slice, a small segment is all such glimpses are. Perversion is only a tiny part of sex which itself is only a part of the human relationship between man and woman. From the ads for the films you might conclude that everyone is queer but "me and thee."

What bothers me is that young people may accept the abnormal for the norm. Often they agree with the subtitle, "What a rotten world we live in."

97

Drama needs conflict, and no one is going to write a drama about civic minded men and women giving hours of their time and much of their money to help underprivileged children. There doesn't seem to be much pulsating excitement in family devotion, love of God and country, protection of the individual by a marvelous code of laws, and other bulwarks of the world we live in. But they exist.

Who will tell our children if the communications media do not? Perhaps parents. Perhaps we can get across the idea that a "slice of life" may be a slice from the rotten part like the spot on the apple—a sound apple which went into the good, juicy pie. Maybe we should tell them that there is much more sweet than bitter.

Do not be conformed to this world but be transformed by the renewal of your mind, that you may prove what is the will of God.

Romans 12:2

God, lead us as parents to look for the good that is in the world and contribute to it instead of accepting the glibly cynical view of a worldly age. Renew our minds that we may radiate the love and the good life of Jesus in our world.

98

Housecleaning
and Heartcleaning

Back in the days of my childhood, every home-maker went through a frantic, frenzied period known as spring housecleaning.

Especially was this true where we lived, in South St. Louis, where the "scrubbin' Dutch" earned their name by scouring stone steps, hanging mattresses out the window and rugs on the clothesline, to be beaten briskly with wire whisks.

Large supplies of wallpaper cleaner were purchased and rolled into pink-turning-gray wads, as we carefully erased the traces of coal smoke from the walls. Mama and Aunt Olie "washed paints," cleaning every mark from the woodwork. Bedspreads were dusted, lace curtains washed and stretched, and everything shone.

Whatever happened to spring housecleaning? It's as out of date as the carpet beater and the feather-bed. The substance used to clean wallpaper has long since been made into play putty for children to use creatively at nursery school. The lace curtain is back, but it's made of miracle, drip-dry, no-iron fabric. Even the front steps have sunk into the ground and become the parking area or the patio outdoor living room.

The reason we no longer have spring cleaning is that, theoretically at least, no house ever gets dirty anymore.

"I don't do spring cleaning," the model housewife says smugly. "My house is always clean."

And a depressing number of homes seem to be that way. The magazines on the coffee table are always in order, stacked according to size and color scheme. The floors are waxed, and every tiny speck of dirt is hastily picked up with a cellulose sponge before it has a chance to cling. Heat doesn't create dust, and if a small amount seeps in from outside, a hole in the wall draws it magically away.

A great portion of our time is devoted to achieving this meticulous ideal. Were a visitor from Mars to study our television commercials or our magazine ads, he would assume that cleanliness is not just next to godliness but way ahead.

Housecleaning brings with it a therapeutic satisfaction. We feel cleaner after finally throwing out the stack of newspapers and magazines we hoped to read some day. Our eyes shine brighter in the reflections from the sparkling windows we just washed.

It's like cleaning the heart. We need that more than housecleaning, for the accumulation of hurts and hostilities, of guilts and jealousies and resentments and lies disturb us much more than a little dust. We are fortunate that God makes heartcleaning easy. He invites us to bring our faults and mistakes to him in open confession so he can cleanse us with his forgiving grace. His forgiveness is sure in Jesus Christ who took our guilt with him to the cross.

Create in me a clean heart, O God, and put a new and right spirit within me.

Psalm 51:10

Lord, make us to be more concerned with clean hearts than with clean houses. We confess that often our living rooms are spotless and our hearts are full of evil. Forgive us, and cleanse us, gracious Father, through the forgiveness of Christ.

What's Your Lifestyle?

Lifestyle. That's a word much in vogue today. The furniture salesman no longer asks you the period you're using in home decoration but the lifestyle you prefer. The young are especially taken with the word. It means, I gather, the way you live, putting your personal mark on your environment, such as framing all the family photographs or hanging your child's crayon drawings.

What is my lifestyle? A good question to ask.

Mine is harried, in a word. Harried and hurried, in two words.

There's a verse I clipped and put on the bulletin board in the kitchen of my new house. It was supposed to set the tone for my new lifestyle in a smaller home in the country. A friend was looking at it one night and I explained its purpose.

"I put it there as a reminder," I said. "It's a poem. It begins, 'Slow me down, O Lord.' I haven't had time to read the rest of it."

It took me a minute to realize why she was laughing.

Those of us who have a lifestyle of being harried, hurried, in a flap, in a twit, ever involved, really like it that way or we wouldn't live that way. There's another prayer I want to put on the bulletin board when I have time: "God grant me the serenity to accept the things I cannot change, the courage to change the things I can, and the wisdom to know the difference."

Maybe another prayer would be for honesty to admit what we really don't want to change.

Most of us would like to change, most of all, the system of priorities under which we operate. Give more time to important things, to home, children, loved ones.

My lifestyle is pretty well child-oriented, to use another catchphrase of our times. I try to listen, accept, understand, and it's my good fortune that the youth I listen to doesn't have any ideas so foreign to my own that I can't accept and understand them.

"Don't sweat the little stuff" is an expression of his generation, inelegant but good advice. My lifestyle seems to devote an inordinate amount of time to trivia, "little stuff." I have to remind myself that it could be stripped on non-essentials.

It really isn't too important if the slipcover lady comes to take the measurements on Friday instead of Thursday. Even if the slipcover isn't ready for the next party, it's no calamity. There will be other parties. If the picnic is rained out, there'll be other picnics. Rained-out ones, too.

Lifestyle. It's made up of so much, the accumulated experiences of our many years and the inherited attitudes of our parents and even the nationality of our ancestors. How to change the inflexible mold we let ourselves get set into? Perhaps by asking, "Is this the style I want for the rest of my life?"

Christ had a lifestyle. Loving people. Putting them first. A good lifestyle for any time. He can make our lifestyle more relevant to today.

Have this mind among yourselves, which you have in Christ Jesus.

Philippians 2:5

Lord God, slowly, painfully, a little at a time, I begin to understand the important things of life. Help me to pattern my ways after those of Jesus Christ, to attain his lifestyle.

Another Chance

A savings and loan company is on the way I travel every day to work. It has a marquee type sign with messages which change weekly. One that struck me in the latter part of December read, "Join Our Christmas Club. Prevent This Year's Mistakes."

Each day I read it and each day I smiled a little ruefully as the thought crossed my mind that it would take more than a Christmas Club to help me prevent all the mistakes I made in this past year.

A Christmas Club account is a great help, of course. Mine matured just in time to help me with a great many mistakes of an overly expansive nature. If nothing else, a savings plan can help you with your financial mistakes of overconfidence.

But then, there are all those other mistakes. The ones you'd just as soon not think about and the ones you can't help thinking about because they are before your eyes.

There are the sins of omission and the sins of commission. There are the deeds described so well by St. Paul. "For I do not do the good I want, but the evil I do not want is what I do." In brief, the all too human sins of human nature.

Try to blot them out. Erase them. Cover them over with whitewash. They're still on the record.

The angry word. The hot retort. The cold reply. The gossipy morsel. The blown top. The indifferent attitude. The lie told. And sometimes, even worse, the truth.

There's nothing you can do to change the mistakes you made in the past. All you can do is try to make amends and apologize. And most important, accept the forgiveness God offers in Christ. Love may mean never having to say you're sorry, but loving means being willing to say you're sorry.

Yesterday's mistakes are there, but thank goodness we have another chance. That's what a new day and a new year are for—a new chance to help you avoid this year's—last year's—mistakes. To take the clean slate and write on it, "I will try to be a better girl—boy—friend—mother—child—wife—husband—lover—human being."

It's okay to open the Christmas Club account,

but don't expect it to do everything. Invest a little in the emotional ledger, too, and trust God to help you avoid repeating mistakes you made in the past.

Better still, let the Spirit of Christ fill your heart with forgiveness for the unavoidable mistakes of the other person.

As the Lord has forgiven you,
so you also must forgive. Colossians 3:13

Lord, I keep making mistakes, often the same mistakes. I never learn. Forgive me and help me start afresh, pick myself up, try again, and come closer to the kind of person you want me to be.

Each Woman
in Her Time

Who are you?

The average woman reacts to this question in a variety of ways, depending on the time, the place, and the circumstances.

At a company dinner for her husband's firm, she says, "I'm Mrs. Smith, John's wife." At a PTA meeting, she says, "I'm Jacky Smith's mother—Miss Johnson's room, Fifth Grade." And if called away from scouring the oven, defrosting the freezer, or digging soggy leaves out of the clogged gutter, she might say with a touch of understandable bitterness, "I'm chief flunky around here, that's who I am."

At a convention of home economists one year, a questionnaire was passed around the delegates, most of them married women with families as well as professionals in their field. It asked the delegates questions about their work and their goals. One question was: "Who are you? List in rate of rank importance your role as home economist or career woman, wife, mother, woman, individual, friend, daughter, etc."

The correct answer, the women were later told, was, "Individual." A woman is supposed to think of herself as an individual first and then as wife, mother, career woman, and the rest.

Maybe so, and yet it seems to me that at 7 a.m. when you're scooping socks up off the floor, scraping burned toast, and answering the wild cry of, "Are my gym clothes dry yet?" it would be difficult to think of yourself as anything but mother first.

Then, too, your answer would depend on the age and stage of life. A new bride would think of herself as wife, the woman with a newborn baby as mother.

Each woman in her time plays many parts, and the roles change, sometimes gradually, sometimes with abrupt and stunning impact. Children grow up and leave home, and you are mother by long distance telephone. Your husband dies, and you are no longer a wife.

Perhaps a part of the dilemma of being a woman in today's world is this fragmentation of our personalities. We always belong a little to someone else, never wholly to ourselves. Who am I? The woman whose usefulness to others has ended may be inclined to answer sadly, "I'm no one, really."

This is not true. Each of us is not only an individual but an individual child of God, not limited to home and family but a human being of unlimited potential, not someone whose place is in home or office or community alone but in God's kingdom, ever pressing toward the mark of our high calling as his servants.

I press on toward the goal for the prize of the upward call of God in Christ Jesus.

Philippians 3:14

O Lord, when the world seems small and oppressive, expand our vision to see the broad horizons of the life you have given us. Keep us from complaining and stir us to greater expression of our vocation as your servants.

Is Any Prayer Too Trivial?

We were on our way to Mexico, the first day on the road when my son casually mentioned that we'd need "proof of ownership" of our car in order to take it across the border.

Of course we would. We'd need the title. And I'd forgotten it. This was the first trip I'd taken to Mexico since my husband was gone and I'd forgotten this essential detail he always handled. What to do?

What we did was to call home when we stopped for the night. Luckily I knew where the title was filed away, and I asked my father to call one of our helpful neighbors to take it to the post office and send it air mail general delivery to a town along the way where we'd be stopping the next night.

The only catch was that the letter wasn't waiting for us when we arrived the next night.

Now rationally I knew it was due to a delay in the mails but emotionally there was only one thing to do. Take it to the Lord in prayer.

"Lord, I hate to bother you with trivial things," I began, "but this isn't trivial to the young people traveling with me. It seems a shame to punish them for my stupidity. Please, Lord, send that title along tomorrow morning."

And in the morning it was there.

All went well. We reached our destination. But then the weather failed to cooperate. Our second day at the beach resort we'd been dreaming of all the long cold winter, and it rained. The next morning it was still raining.

"Lord, I know I promised you I'd never pray about the weather again," I found myself saying. "It's such a trivial matter. And for myself it really wouldn't matter. I could stay indoors and knit and read and relax and listen to the pounding of the surf, but the young people need the status of that suntan. Lord, if you could just send this storm out to sea and bring back the beautiful sunshine."

Cynics would say that tropical storms clear up in a hurry. All I can say is that the sun was shining by noon.

I feel a little ashamed when I pray these trivial prayers. I know that prayers should be those of a

112

thankful heart or prayers of importance—for peace and brotherhood—or prayers asking for guidance, not the "gimme" sort of prayers or prayers for special favors. Yet what woman doesn't pray to have her son accepted by a certain college, or for an evening's popularity at the party for her daughter, or for the easing of heartache, or worldly success for someone who is near to her.

For good or not, our prayers are trivial prayers. I only hope he understands.

If you ask anything in my name, I will do it.

John 14:14

Lord, give us faith to be concerned for more than little things. But thank you for letting us feel that no problem is too small to bring to you in prayer.

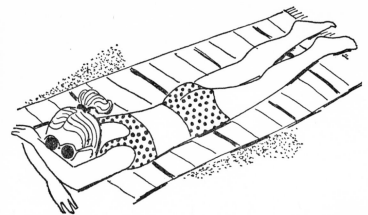

Home Is Where
the Action Is

"I want to go to Japan and work on a newspaper there before I succumb to the dull life of the house-wife."

These words bounced out of a story on the women's page of a newspaper. The story was about Holly Hoffmeister, first woman reporter in 93 years on the staff of the Princeton University newspaper.

Now normally girl reporters stick together, but this is a case in which I believe the wisdom of age should correct the mistaken impression of the young.

The life of a housewife dull? O Holly, you have spent too much time in the halls of ivy and too little observing the exciting, often dangerous world of the homemaker.

Were James Bond's hero 007 to exchange places with Mrs. Milbert Milquetoast of 700 Fertile Acres

114

for just one day, preferably a rainy Monday, he would gladly return to the comparative calm of flashing knives and vials of poison.

A Cadillac that fires ballistic missiles from the headlights is nothing compared to a car pool of children on their way home from nursery school. I wish I hadn't brought the subject up because it calls to mind that adorable little girl who loved to release the handbrake when we parked on top of a steep hill.

The life of a housewife dull? Holly, you have no idea of the endlessly changing and colorful pattern of a day at home.

Have you ever known the surging, pulsating sensation of having a washing machine overflow onto the freshly painted basement floor to which the cat was stuck by her paws? Have you ever left a flaming oven of steak grease to respond to a piercing scream from the playroom? Or battled 17 wasps that flew down the chimney of the family room just before a dinner party?

I've worked on a newspaper, and I've worked at home, and for sheer peril, home wins by a migraine mile. What excitement of an interview could compare with driving up to the Cub Scout mothers' tea to be told, "You'd better go right to the hospital. One of the mothers was walking along the street and she saw this child all covered with blood. . . ."

No headline or deadline drama could hold a candle to the moment when I stood on the attic ladder trying to get a skylight back in place (someone had been sunbathing on the roof) before the rains brought the ceiling down. Emblazoned in my book of memory is that moment when I relaxed to lean against the stair rail but looked around just in time. There is no stair rail.

Don't get me wrong though, Holly. Housewifery isn't all burning toast and prunes, exploding appliances, and things that go bump and burp in the night. There's a feature called a husband. If you find the right one, life really isn't at all dull.

She looks well to the ways of her household, and does not eat the bread of idleness.

Proverbs 31:27

Lord God, sometimes we homemakers find our days dull, our lives tedious, our time consumed with a myriad of little things which seem of little importance. Help us to see our true worth, our value as people, and our place in that most important of all places—the home.

Go It While You're Young

I wonder if young people realize how beautiful they look to the elderly, that is, the past 30-year-old observer. Probably not. Young people are terribly critical in appraising the appearance of their peers and positive in their judgments. This one is "sharp" or "a doll," but that one is "a mess." As for their own appearances, they see nothing good at all. Lost on them is the clear level gaze, the firm fresh skin, the lean coltish grace. They see only the nose a fraction too long or too short, the freckle, the bump, the hair out of line—and they despair.

I thought of all this one day when a group of boys and girls from the high school choir sang at our church luncheon. It was a Christmas party, and they sang not religious carols but the more secular ones. There are those who decry the singing of anything but religious carols; however, these were so gay that they put all of us in a holiday spirit.

They sang about "Rudolph, the Red-Nosed Reindeer" with pantomime and sound effects, and "Have Yourself a Merry Little Christmas," and "The Twelve Days of Christmas," getting breathless as they raced through the final recital of "my true love's" generosity.

They sang "Sleigh Ride," the boys hugging the girls with some giggling and self-consciousness, and then they sang "Jingle Bells" with its old fashioned lyrics: "Now the ground is white—go it while you're young."

Looking at the beautiful young people, I recalled a conversation with some contemporaries. We'd been looking through an old high school yearbook and talking about, "Whatever happened to—?" It was a little sad. So many of the bright hopes faded, the young lives snuffed out in wars, the gallant dreams ground down on the wheels of humdrum living.

The beautiful young people, so fresh-faced and gay—you wonder what is ahead for them. Most of the biblical admonitions hold out little hope for continuing joy. They admonish the young man to be joyous in his youth but warn him that a day of reckoning will come.

It is true that no life is without its share of sorrow, and yet there is a place for joy, too, for the carefree happy pleasure of simply being alive— and young. The parent longs to help them enjoy the "now," not in a fatalistic, pagan manner, but in a joyful, grateful way, loving them each day and forming lasting good memories for them.

Life can be frantic, frenetic, fretful for the homemaker. It should be as busy as it often is. We should not let birthdays and Christmas and family festivals go by without real celebration, with songs and laughter and love, all of us, all ages.

As for the beautiful young people—go it while you're young.

Rejoice, O young man, in your youth, and let your heart cheer you in the days of your youth.

Ecclesiastes 11:9

God, be good to them, our tender and vulnerable young. Give them high hopes for the future, a plan for a life of service and even sacrifice, but now, in their youth, also give them joy.

The Family Room

The criers of doom tell us we're seeing the breakdown of the family. The younger generation has revolted. They're off doing their own "thing." The older generation has been shunted away, put on the shelf. As for us in the middle years, who needs us? Who trusts anyone over 30? Who admits to being 40? Every woman is just "39 and holding."

And yet this is the era that has seen the rise of the "family room"—a unit of the household quite different from grandma's "best parlor," from the "living room" of the bungalow of the 1920s.

A television ad aims its appeal at the ecological generation by stressing "a return to basics." The family room is a return to basics, too. A return to the past.

"We call our family room the 'keeping room,'" a lover of antiques said to me. "That's what they called the main room of the house in Colonial times, you know."

It would be an appropriate name for the family room of our house, too. For the family room of many homes. We keep everything from birdseed to baseball bats, snowgear to swimming supplies in our family room.

Our family room is on the "road to" more places than Bing Crosby and Bob Hope in their movie heyday.

It's on the road to the out of doors so it's the ideal place to park full wastebaskets and stacks of old newspapers until they can be taken out.

It's on the road to the play area for children and the road into the house for dogs. This is how footballs and bones end up side by side at the doorway.

It's a way station for dying plants, wilted flower arrangements, candle stubs, and stacks of magazines with pretty pictures which I mean to clip and file away some day. Why? So we could have a family room like the pretty pictures instead of the keeping room we have.

But never mind. The important thing about our family room is that the family is often there. It's the breakfast room, so it's where we say grace before meals. It's the place for the Advent wreath before

Christmas. It's the late night quiet place where confidences are exchanged and plans made as the firelight flickers and flames up again.

And somehow I can't believe the criers of doom who foretell the breakdown of the family as I see the homes with family rooms—and the families who make a place for God in their homes.

The eternal God is your dwelling place, and underneath are the everlasting arms.

Deuteronomy 33:27

God and Father, come into our homes, fine or humble as they may be. Make our dwelling place your dwelling place and make its foundation your everlasting arms.

Morals and Marigolds

"I've finally come into my own," said a friend of mine, a maiden lady who does not like to be described as such.

"I don't have any children, so I'm not contributing to the population explosion. I don't drive a car, so I'm not polluting the atmosphere. I recirculate my newspapers and I bury my garbage. I'd been burying my garbage after dark," she continued. "That was so the neighbors wouldn't know what made the roses so big and also wouldn't report me to the health department. Now I find I'm doing just what good ecology practices recommend."

I, too, was an early bloomer, and I, too, try to follow the rules. Since I have moved to the country, it's relatively easy. With no garbage disposal, it's necessary to bury the garbage. With no trash pick-up, it's desirable to recirculate the no-return bottles, which I do, taking them to a nearby suburban pick-up point, where I separate them as to color and toss them into the right bin. Sometimes there's even a therapeutic effect as we are encouraged to break the bottles, and there's nothing like a good shattering smash to ease tensions.

Many of the glass recycling projects are in the hands of young people, and I think it's great that they are taking this interest in cleaning up the mess our land is in.

I must confess to a certain amount of annoyance when young people act as if they invented concern for ecology and environment. Many years ago garden clubbers and other nature lovers began working on what was then called "conservation." There were anti-litter campaigns and anti-billboard campaigns before these youths dropped their first candy wrapper on the street.

And while paying lipservice to a cleaner country and coming out forthrightly against the industrial establishment, some of them are still not too personally involved, as the litter after a rock festival or the clutter of their rooms indicates. If only we mothers could get them to recycle their socks—separating them by color and using them again and again.

Meanwhile, ecology is "in" for young and old. We women try to observe all the rules, to buy the proper detergent (which turns out a few weeks later to have been the improper detergent), to practice organic, non-chemical gardening (until the

124

bagworms descend) and to us grandmother's trick of planting marigolds around the roses and the tomatoes to discourage the insects.

What do marigolds have to do with morals? Quite a bit. In coming to grips with the ecological problems of our times—pollution, litter, despoiling the land—and in trying to beautify our own surroundings, we are obeying our Lord's commandments that we love God and love our neighbor.

To love God is to respect his beautiful world. To love our neighbor is to show respect and consideration for the air he breathes, the water he drinks, the countryside he enjoys.

Perhaps the interest of young people in nature is less a rejection of their parents 'materialism than a desire to get back to basic values, to things that will not rust or corrode—or self destruct. To return to the places where Jesus preached his words —by the sea, in the garden, and under the sky.

Whatever you wish that men would do to you, do so to them; for this is the law and the prophets.
Matthew 7:12

Lord, help us to keep pure and beautiful the world of your creation. Make us see that concern for nature is the highest form of concern for our fellow man.

125

His Resurrection
Really Happened

Once upon a time when you were young, or maybe not so young, something wonderful happened. You went out one evening, casually, not realizing what fate had in store, and you met someone you'd known only in your dreams. And the world splintered into sparklers and stardust. And the next morning you woke up and said to yourself, "It happened—it really happened."

That's the way I feel about the resurrection of Jesus Christ. "It happened—it really happened." We celebrate his resurrection every Sunday, but I'm glad we have a special Easter festival to celebrate this greatest of all events.

So many of the celebrations we family managers plan and execute are made up of tribal rites, tradition, folk customs, and fairy tales that it's easy to forget when we're celebrating pure truth.

Christmas is Santa Claus and reindeer skimming over the rooftops and jolly elves in the toy shop at the North Pole.

It's the birth of Baby Jesus, of course, but this is as stylized as the nativity scene under the tree surrounded by cotton snow, and we remember it in a way it didn't quite happen.

Then we come to Easter and new clothes and Peter Cottontail hopping down the bunny trail. It's Easter, the high feast day of the church, and baskets of colored eggs, and ham or lamb for dinner, and spring is really here even if it rains.

When all the time we should be thinking that tremulous thought—it really happened. Not a "happening" by present day standards. Not a happenstance. Not a myth, a story, or a folk tale, but something tangible, substantiated by witnesses. Many witnesses, as Paul described them, "five hundred brethren . . . most of whom are still alive."

Louis Cassels, newspaper columnist, says of the Gospel accounts of Christ's life and death and resurrection, "If UPI had four different reporters covering a running story that extended over as much time and territory as the life of Christ, we'd feel that they had done an extraordinary good job if their accounts dovetailed as well as the Gospels."

Even so, many of us who accept as gospel truth what we read in today's newspapers, think of the greatest story, "It would be nice if it were true." We would like to believe except for our unbelief.

Easter is our day to celebrate the truth of Jesus' resurrection. His victory over death means that he has taken the sting out of our death. Because he conquered death, we die in the faith that we will be with him forever.

Thanks be to God, who gives us the victory through our Lord Jesus Christ.

I Corinthians 15:57

Lord, help us to know and to celebrate the power of your resurrection. Strengthen our faith to live in your victory over evil and death. Keep alive in us the hope of our resurrection.